Scott Foresman
Reading

Kindergarten

Phonics
Take-Home
Readers

Scott Foresman
Phonics System

Scott Foresman

Editorial Offices: Glenview, Illinois • New York, New York
Sales Offices: Reading, Massachusetts • Duluth, Georgia • Glenview, Illinois
Carrollton, Texas • Menlo Park, California

Editorial Offices
Glenview, Illinois • New York, New York

Sales Offices
Reading, Massachusetts • Duluth, Georgia • Glenview, Illinois
Carrollton, Texas • Menlo Park, California

ISBN 0-673-61257-0

3 4 5 6 7 8 9 10-CRK-06 05 04 03 02 01 00

TABLE OF CONTENTS

Phonics Readers for Unit 5

Phonics Readers for Unit 6

Scott Foresman
Reading

Kindergarten
Phonics Reader 1

ABC Stories
by Cora Plexus
illustrated by
Kate Flanagan

Phonics Skills:
• Readiness
• Alphabetical order

Scott Foresman
Phonics System

Scott Foresman

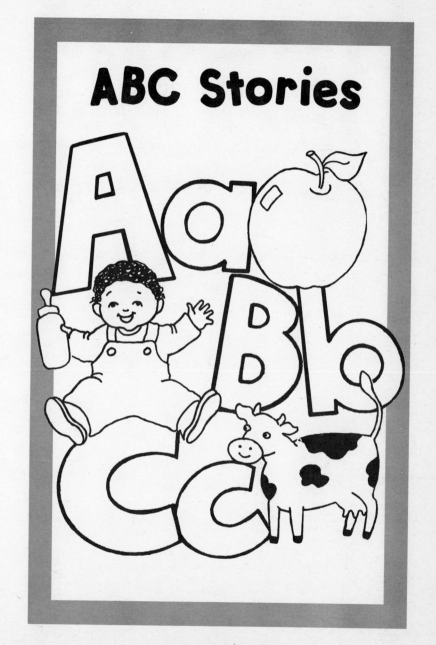

ABC Stories

by Cora Plexus
illustrated by Kate Flanagan

This book belongs to

_____

Phonics for Families: Look at the scenes in this book with your child and encourage him or her to tell a story about each scene. Then go back through the book, choosing one letter at a time, and have your child find things in the picture whose names begin with that letter.

Phonics Skills: Readiness; Alphabetical order

W   X   Y   Z

w   x   y   z

ABC Stories

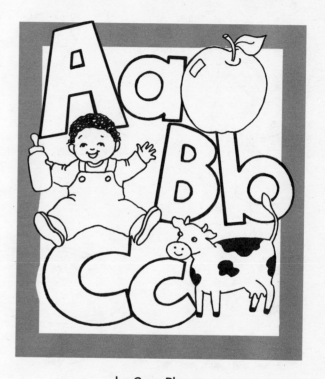

by Cora Plexus

illustrated by Kate Flanagan

Scott Foresman

Editorial Offices: Glenview, Illinois • New York, New York
Sales Offices: Reading, Massachusetts • Duluth, Georgia
Glenview, Illinois • Carrollton, Texas • Menlo Park, California

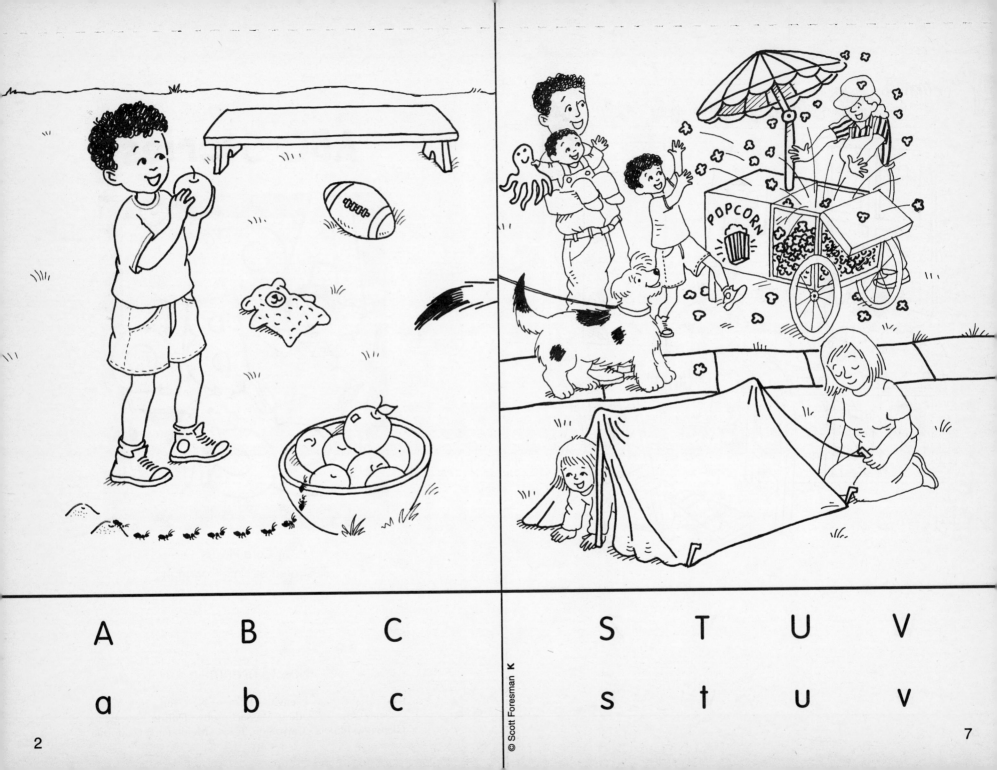

A   B   C

a   b   c

2

S   T   U   V

s   t   u   v

7

O   P   Q   R   D   E   F

o   p   q   r   d   e   f

G H I J

g h i j

K L M N

k l m n

Scott Foresman
Reading

Kindergarten
Phonics Reader 2

Meet My Family
by Merrily Hansen
illustrated by
Tom Barrett

Phonics Skill:
• Rhyming

Scott Foresman
Phonics System

Scott Foresman

by Merrily Hansen
illustrated by Tom Barrett

This book belongs to

_____

Phonics for Families: This rhyming book uses a repetitive pattern with the high-frequency words *is* and *like*. Take turns reading aloud. Invite your child to name people in your family and tell what he or she likes to do with each family member.

Phonics Skill: Rhyming

High-Frequency Words: *like, is*

This is my family.

See what we do.

We like to play.

How about you?

8

Meet My Family

by Merrily Hansen
illustrated by Tom Barrett

Scott Foresman

Editorial Offices: Glenview, Illinois • New York, New York
Sales Offices: Reading, Massachusetts • Duluth, Georgia
Glenview, Illinois • Carrollton, Texas • Menlo Park, California

This is my mom.

We like to dig.

We go to the park.

We have so much fun.

This is my sister.
We like to run.

We water the flowers.
They get so big.

This is my dad.
We like to cook.

We make big pancakes.
How do they look?

Scott Foresman
Reading

**Kindergarten
Phonics Reader 3**

My Mitten
by Maryann Dobeck
illustrated by
Lisa Zolnowski

Phonics Skill:
• Initial consonant *m*

Scott Foresman
**Phonics
System**

Scott Foresman

My Mitten

by Maryann Dobeck
illustrated by Lisa Zolnowski

This book belongs to

_____

Phonics for Families: This book gives your child practice in reading words that begin with *m*, as in *mouse*, and the high-frequency words *am* and *can*. After reading the book together, help your child identify the objects in the pictures whose names begin with *m*.

Phonics Skill: Initial consonant *m*

High-Frequency Words: *am, can*

Me!

My Mitten

by Maryann Dobeck
illustrated by Lisa Zolnowski

Scott Foresman

Editorial Offices: Glenview, Illinois • New York, New York
Sales Offices: Reading, Massachusetts • Duluth, Georgia
Glenview, Illinois • Carrollton, Texas • Menlo Park, California

I am going out.

Where is my mitten?

2

Who can find my mitten?

7

Is my mitten on the map?

Is my mitten on the mouse?

Is my mitten on the monkey?

Is my mitten on the mop?

Scott Foresman
Reading

Kindergarten
Phonics Reader 4

My Red Bike
by Robyn Silbey
illustrated by
Dennis Hockerman

Phonics Skill:
• Initial consonant *r*

Scott Foresman
Phonics System

Scott Foresman

My Red Bike

by Robyn Silbey
illustrated by Dennis Hockerman

This book belongs to

_____

© Scott Foresman K

Phonics for Families: This book gives your child practice in reading words that begin with *r*, as in *rock*, and the high-frequency words *blue* and *red*. Read the book together. Then go on a search around your home, looking for objects whose names begin with *r*.

Phonics Skill: Initial consonant *r*
High-Frequency Words: *blue, red*

I give my blue bike to Rob.

8

My Red Bike

by Robyn Silbey
illustrated by Dennis Hockerman

Scott Foresman

Editorial Offices: Glenview, Illinois • New York, New York
Sales Offices: Reading, Massachusetts • Duluth, Georgia
Glenview, Illinois • Carrollton, Texas • Menlo Park, California

Here is a red bike for me!

I ride home.

I ride to the rabbits.

I ride my red bike.

I ride to the rock.

I ride to the red barn.

Kindergarten
Phonics Reader 5

Six Sisters
by Susana Vasquez
illustrated by
Geneviève LeLoup

Phonics Skills:
• Initial consonant *s*

Scott Foresman
Phonics System

Scott Foresman

Six Sisters

by Susana Vasquez
illustrated by Geneviève LeLoup

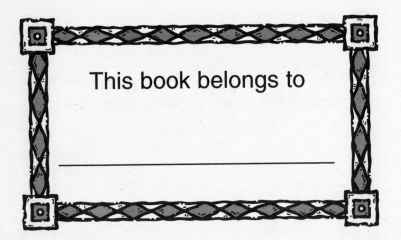

This book belongs to

_____

Phonics for Families: This book gives your child practice reading words that begin with *s*, as in *sit*. Read the book together. Then encourage your child to name words that have the same beginning sound as *sit*.

Phonics Skill: Initial consonant *s*

Sister number seven.

8

Six Sisters

by Susana Vasquez
illustrated by Geneviève LeLoup

Scott Foresman

Editorial Offices: Glenview, Illinois • New York, New York
Sales Offices: Reading, Massachusetts • Duluth, Georgia
Glenview, Illinois • Carrollton, Texas • Menlo Park, California

We are six sisters.

What?

But we feel so, so sad.

We miss something.

We sit on the sand.

We see the sails.

4

We sing some songs.

5

Scott Foresman
Reading

Kindergarten
Phonics Reader 6

Monkey Fun
by Jenny Della Penna
illustrated by
Tim Haggerty

Phonics Review:
• Initial consonants

Scott Foresman
Phonics
System

Scott Foresman

Monkey Fun

by Jenny Della Penna
illustrated by Tim Haggerty

This book belongs to

_____

Phonics for Families: This book reviews words that begin with *m*, *r*, and *s*, as in *mop*, *run*, and *sing*. Read the book together. Then invite your child to name and act out other activities that begin with *m*, *r*, and *s*.

Phonics Skill: Initial consonants

Six monkeys have fun!

8

Monkey Fun

by Jenny Della Penna
illustrated by Tim Haggerty

Scott Foresman

Editorial Offices: Glenview, Illinois • New York, New York
Sales Offices: Reading, Massachusetts • Duluth, Georgia
Glenview, Illinois • Carrollton, Texas • Menlo Park, California

Six monkeys read.

Six monkeys mix.

Six monkeys run.

Six monkeys mop.

Six monkeys rake.

Six monkeys sing.

Scott Foresman
Reading

Kindergarten
Phonics Reader 7

Bears
by Anastasia Suen

Phonics Skill:
• Initial consonant *b*

Scott Foresman
Phonics System

Scott Foresman

Bears

by Anastasia Suen

This book belongs to

_____

© Scott Foresman **K**

Phonics for Families: This book features words that begin with *b*, as in *bears*, and the high-frequency words *but* and *I*. Invite your child to read the book aloud. Then have your child point out the objects in the pictures that begin with *b*.

Phonics Skill: Initial consonant *b*

High-Frequency Words: *but, I*

But I am not a bear.
I am a boy!

8

Bears

by Anastasia Suen

Scott Foresman

Editorial Offices: Glenview, Illinois • New York, New York
Sales Offices: Reading, Massachusetts • Duluth, Georgia
Glenview, Illinois • Carrollton, Texas • Menlo Park, California

Bears play.

I sleep too.

Bears sleep.

I play too.

Bears swim.

I swim too.

Scott Foresman
Reading

Kindergarten
Phonics Reader 8

Tom Gets Wet
by Ada Eveyln
illustrated by
Valeria Petrone

Phonics Skill:
• Initial and final
  consonant *t*

Scott Foresman
Phonics System

Scott Foresman

Tom Gets Wet

by Ada Evelyn
illustrated by Valeria Petrone

This book belongs to

_____

Phonics for Families: This book provides practice reading words that begin or end with *t*, as in *Tom* and *wet*. Read the book aloud with your child. Then ask your child to find the words that begin or end with the *t* sound.

Phonics Skill: Initial and final consonant *t*

8

Tom Gets Wet

by Ada Evelyn
illustrated by Valeria Petrone

Scott Foresman

Editorial Offices: Glenview, Illinois • New York, New York
Sales Offices: Reading, Massachusetts • Duluth, Georgia
Glenview, Illinois • Carrollton, Texas • Menlo Park, California

4

5

Kindergarten
Phonics Reader 9

Rat at Bat
by Cathy East Dubowski
and Mark Dubowski
illustrated by
Cameron Eagle

Phonics Skill:
• Short *a*

Scott Foresman

by Cathy East Dubowski and Mark Dubowski
illustrated by Cameron Eagle

This book belongs to

_____

Phonics for Families: This book gives your child practice in reading words with short *a* and the high-frequency words *go* and *the*. Read the book together. Then ask your child to name words that rhyme with *rat*.

Phonics Skill: Short *a*

High-Frequency Words: *go, the*

Hooray for Rat!

You **can** bat!

8

Rat at Bat

by Cathy East Dubowski and Mark Dubowski
illustrated by Cameron Eagle

Scott Foresman

Editorial Offices: Glenview, Illinois • New York, New York
Sales Offices: Reading, Massachusetts • Duluth, Georgia
Glenview, Illinois • Carrollton, Texas • Menlo Park, California

Go, Rat!

Put on your cap!

CRACK

You can do it!

Yes, you can!

Oh, no, Rat!
Do not get mad!

6

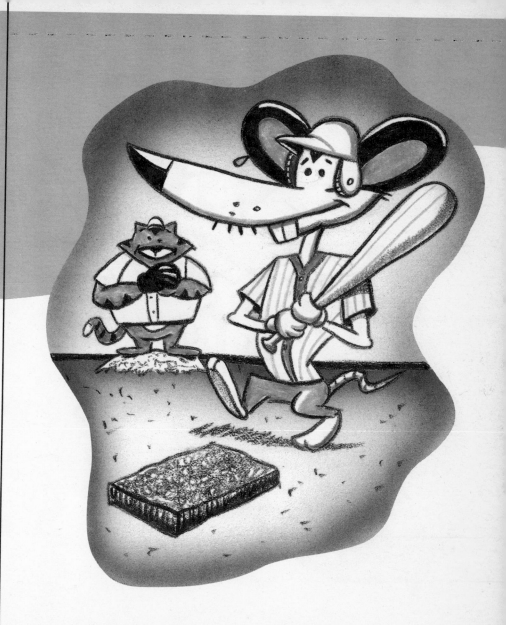

Go to the mat!
Get ready to bat!

3

Tap, tap, tap your bat!

Tap your bat on the mat!

Oh, no, Rat!

Do not be sad!

Scott Foresman Reading

Kindergarten
Phonics Reader 10

Fifi and Fido
by Susan Whitney
illustrated by
Doug Roy

Phonics Skill:
• Initial consonant f

Scott Foresman
Phonics System

Scott Foresman

Fifi and Fido

by Susan Whitney
illustrated by Doug Roy

This book belongs to

_____

Phonics for Families: This book features words that begin with the *f* sound as in *fox*. Read the book together. Point out the words that begin with the *f* sound. Have your child find objects in the pictures that begin with the *f* sound.

Phonics Skill: Initial consonant *f*

Fido wins!

8

Fifi and Fido

by Susan Whitney
illustrated by Doug Roy

Scott Foresman

Editorial Offices: Glenview, Illinois • New York, New York
Sales Offices: Reading, Massachusetts • Duluth, Georgia
Glenview, Illinois • Carrollton, Texas • Menlo Park, California

Fifi and Fido will run far.

No. Fifi will not.

2

7

Will Fifi get up?

6

Five-mile race today!

How far?
Five miles!

3

Fifi is fast.
Fido is not.

Fifi is hot.
Fido is not.

Kindergarten
Phonics Reader 11

No Nap for Ned
by Joan Cottle
illustrated by
Mark McIntyre

Phonics Skills:
• Initial and final
consonant *n*

No Nap for Ned

by Joan Cottle
illustrated by Mark McIntyre

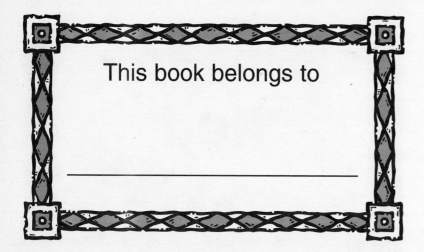

This book belongs to

_____

Phonics for Families: This book provides your child with practice reading words that begin and end with *n*, as in *nap* and *Dan*, and also the high-frequency words *it* and *have*. Read the book aloud and then talk about the pet your child has or might like to have.

Phonics Skill: Initial and final consonant *n*

High-Frequency Words: *it, have*

No! Not now!

No Nap for Ned

by Joan Cottle
illustrated by Mark McIntyre

Scott Foresman

Editorial Offices: Glenview, Illinois • New York, New York
Sales Offices: Reading, Massachusetts • Duluth, Georgia
Glenview, Illinois • Carrollton, Texas • Menlo Park, California

Ned wants to nap.

Does Ned want to nap now?

Ned wants to nap.

Ned wants to nap.

4

5

Scott Foresman
Reading

Kindergarten
Phonics Reader 12

Ted and Nat
by Becky Manfredini
illustrated by
John Margeson

Phonics Review:
• Consonants
• Short *a*

Scott Foresman
Phonics System

Scott Foresman

by Becky Manfredini
illustrated by John Margeson

This book belongs to

_____

Phonics for Families: This book provides your child with practice reading consonants and words that contain short *a*, and the high-frequency words *do* and *not*. After reading the book aloud, encourage your child to suggest what he or she might make with a large box.

Phonics Review: Consonants; Short *a*

High-Frequency Words: *do, not*

I do not.

Ted and Nat

by Becky Manfredini
Illustrated by John Margeson

Scott Foresman

Editorial Offices: Glenview, Illinois • New York, New York
Sales Offices: Reading, Massachusetts • Duluth, Georgia
Glenview, Illinois • Carrollton, Texas • Menlo Park, California

Ted makes a boat.

Ted has fun.

2

7

Nat makes a seesaw.

Nat has fun.

Nat sits on his mat.

Ted makes a rocket.

Ted has fun.

4

I do not like it.

Nat sits on his mat.

5

Scott Foresman
Reading

Kindergarten
Phonics Reader 13

Where Is Piggy?
by Alexandra Behr
illustrated by
Chuck Gonzales

Phonics Skill:
• Initial and final
  consonant *p*

Scott Foresman
Phonics System

Scott Foresman

by Alexandra Behr
illustrated by Chuck Gonzales

This book belongs to

_____

Phonics for Families This book features words that begin and end with *p*, as in *pig* and *mop*. Read the book with your child. Then have your child point out objects in the book whose names begin or end with the *p* sound.

Phonics Skill: Initial and final consonant *p*

Where Is Piggy?

by Alexandra Behr
Illustrated by Chuck Gonzales

Scott Foresman

Editorial Offices: Glenview, Illinois • New York, New York
Sales Offices: Reading, Massachusetts • Duluth, Georgia
Glenview, Illinois • Carrollton, Texas • Menlo Park, California

Where is Piggy?

Where is Piggy?

Pat looks for Piggy.

Pat finds a pan.

Pat looks for Piggy.

Pat finds a mop.

Pat looks for Piggy.

Pat finds a pot.

Pat looks for Piggy.

Pat finds a cup.

Scott Foresman
Reading

Kindergarten
Phonics Reader 14

A Plan for Nan
by Nat Gabriel
illustrated by
Lane Yerkes

Phonics Skill:
• Short *a*

Scott Foresman
Phonics System

Scott Foresman

A Plan
For Nan

by Nat Gabriel
illustrated by Lane Yerkes

This book belongs to

_____

Phonics for Families: This book provides your child with practice reading words with short *a*, as in *pan*, and the high-frequency words *big* and *in*. Read the book together. Then have your child name words that rhyme with *rat*, *ran*, and *rap*.

Phonics Skill: Short *a*

High-Frequency Words: *in*, *big*

Nan had a big tan fan!

8

A Plan
For Nan

by Nat Gabriel
illustrated by Lane Yerkes

Scott Foresman

Editorial Offices: Glenview, Illinois • New York, New York
Sales Offices: Reading, Massachusetts • Duluth, Georgia
Glenview, Illinois • Carrollton, Texas • Menlo Park, California

Nan had a big pan.

It was too hot!

But Nan had a plan.

Cat, Rat, and Bat sat.
Nan got the big pan.

Tap! Tap!
Cat went in.

Rap! Rap!

Rat ran in.

Tap! Tap!

Rap! Rap!

Bat went in.

Scott Foresman
Reading

Kindergarten
Phonics Reader 15

The Cool Hen
by Ada Evelyn
illustrated by
Lisa Chauncy Guida

Phonics Skill:
• Initial consonant *h*

Scott Foresman
Phonics
System

Scott Foresman

The Cool Hen

by Ada Evelyn
illustrated by Lisa Chauncy Guida

This book belongs to

_____

© Scott Foresman **K**

Phonics for Families: This book features words that begin with *h*, as in *hen*. Read the book aloud with your child. Then ask him or her to point out words that begin with *h*.

Phonics Skill: Initial consonant *h*

Why not?

The Cool Hen

by Ada Evelyn

illustrated by Liisa Chauncy Guida

Scott Foresman

Editorial Offices: Glenview, Illinois • New York, New York
Sales Offices: Reading, Massachusetts • Duluth, Georgia
Glenview, Illinois • Carrollton, Texas • Menlo Park, California

But hen is not hot.

Hop is hot.

It is hot, hot, hot.

Kit is hot.

Red is hot.

Scott Foresman
Reading

Kindergarten
Phonics Reader 16

Gas Helps It Go
by Melissa Blackwell Burke
illustrated by
Donald Cook

Phonics Skill:
• Initial and final
  consonant *g*

Scott Foresman
Phonics System

Scott Foresman

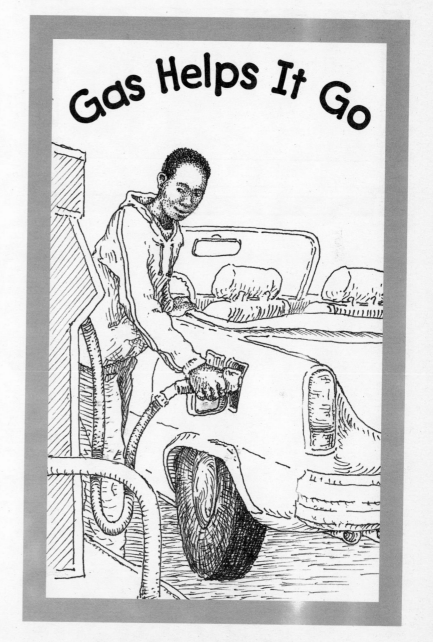

Gas Helps It Go

by Melissa Blackwell Burke
illustrated by Donald Cook

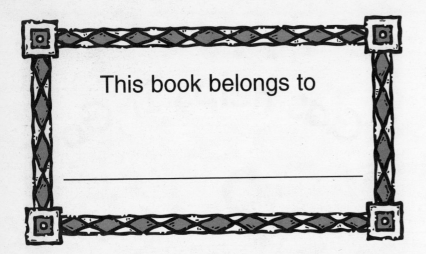

This book belongs to

_____

Phonics for Families: This book gives your child practice in reading words that begin or end with g, as in *gas* and *big*. Read the book together. Then encourage your child to find objects in the pictures whose names begin or end with g.

Phonics Skill: Initial and final consonant g

Today, the big rig gives gas.

Fill it up, please!

8

Gas Helps It Go

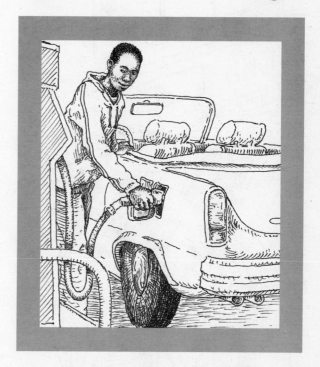

by Melissa Blackwell Burke
illustrated by Donald Cook

Scott Foresman

Editorial Offices: Glenview, Illinois • New York, New York
Sales Offices: Reading, Massachusetts • Duluth, Georgia
Glenview, Illinois • Carrollton, Texas • Menlo Park, California

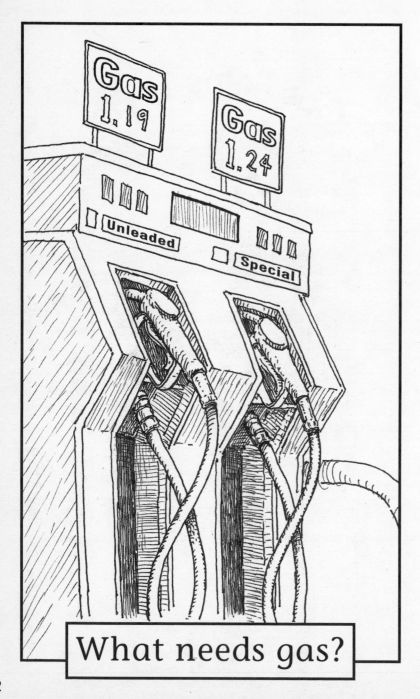

What needs gas?

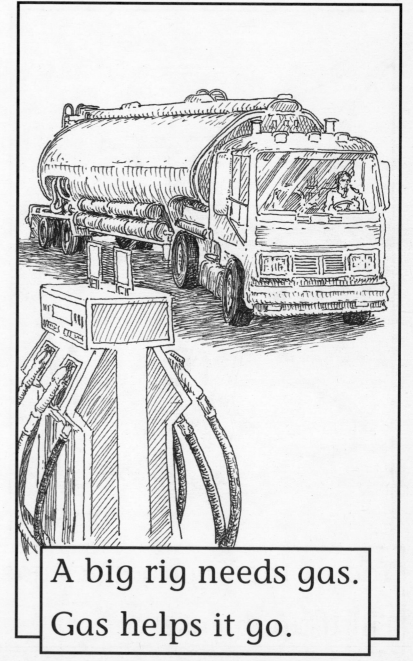

A big rig needs gas.
Gas helps it go.

A van needs gas.
Gas helps it go.

A car needs gas.
Gas helps it go.

A bus needs gas.
Gas helps it go.

A truck needs gas.
Gas helps it go.

Scott Foresman
Reading

Kindergarten
Phonics Reader 17

Pig and the Big Rig
by Judy Nayer
illustrated by
Jeff LeVan

Phonics Skill:
• Short *i*

Scott Foresman
Phonics
System

Scott Foresman

Pig and
the Big Rig

by Judy Nayer
illustrated by Jeff LeVan

This book belongs to

_____

Phonics for Families: This story helps your child read words with short *i* and the high-frequency words *a* and *up*. Read the book to your child. Then have him or her read the book to you. Invite your child to find words that end with *-ig* and *-it*.

Phonics Skill: Short *i*
High-Frequency Words: *a, up*

It is big!

Pig and the Big Rig

by Judy Nayer
illustrated by Jeff LeVan

Scott Foresman

Editorial Offices: Glenview, Illinois • New York, New York
Sales Offices: Reading, Massachusetts • Duluth, Georgia
Glenview, Illinois • Carrollton, Texas • Menlo Park, California

Pig gets up into the big rig.

© Scott Foresman **K**

What is it?

Pig is up the hill.

6

3

No.
But you can jump on it.

What is in the rig, Pig?
Is it a big rug?

© Scott Foresman K

Scott Foresman
Reading

Kindergarten
Phonics Reader 18

The Big Fat Hat
by Dina Anastasio
illustrated by
Esther Szegedy

Phonics Review:
• Consonants
• Short *a*
• Short *i*

Scott Foresman
Phonics System

Scott Foresman

The Big Fat Hat

by Dina Anastasio
illustrated by Esther Szegedy

This book belongs to

_____

Phonics for Families: This book provides your child with practice reading words that contain short *a* and short *i*. Read the book together and then have your child find words in the book that have these short vowel sounds.

Phonics Review: Consonants, Short *a*; Short *i*

8

The Big Fat Hat

by Dina Anastasio

illustrated by Esther Szegedy

Scott Foresman

Editorial Offices: Glenview, Illinois • New York, New York
Sales Offices: Reading, Massachusetts • Duluth, Georgia
Glenview, Illinois • Carrollton, Texas • Menlo Park, California

A big fat hat!

I can use that hat!

The cat!

I can read a map in it.

I can sit in it.

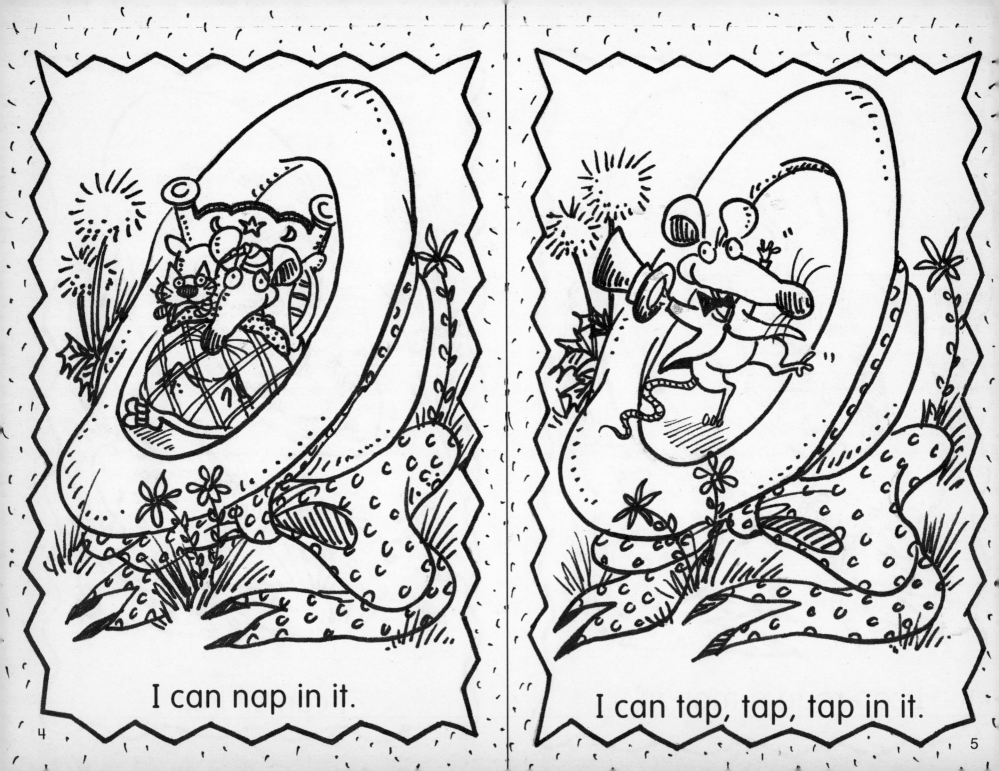

I can nap in it.

I can tap, tap, tap in it.

4

5

Scott Foresman
Reading

Kindergarten
Phonics Reader 19

The Cat in the Cab
by Holly Melton
illustrated by
David Austin Clar

Phonics Skill:
• Initial consonant c

Scott Foresman
Phonics System

Scott Foresman

The Cat in the Cab

by Holly Melton
illustrated by David Austin Clar

This book belongs to

_____

Phonics for Families: This book gives your child practice in reading words that begin with *c*, as in *cab*. It also provides practice reading the high-frequency words *get* and *where*. Read the book together. Then make up a funny cat story together.

Phonics Skill: Initial consonant *c*

High-Frequency Words: *get, where*

Cam is in the cab!

8

The Cat in the Cab

by Holly Melton
illustrated by David Austin Clar

Scott Foresman

Editorial Offices: Glenview, Illinois • New York, New York
Sales Offices: Reading, Massachusetts • Duluth, Georgia
Glenview, Illinois • Carrollton, Texas • Menlo Park, California

Where is my cat?

No Cam?

I have to get Cam!

Oh, no!

Cam is in the cart.

© Scott Foresman K

Where is Cam?

Oh, no!

Cam is in the cab.

4

I have to get Cam!

5

Scott Foresman
Reading

**Kindergarten
Phonics Reader 20**

Dolly Digs
by Linda Yoshizawa
illustrated by
Remy Simard

Phonics Skill:
• Initial Consonant *d*

Scott Foresman
**Phonics
System**

Scott Foresman

Dolly
Digs!

by Linda Yoshizawa
illustrated by Remy Simard

This book belongs to

_____

Phonics for Families: Read the story together. Then have your child name the animal on the cover and listen for *d* at the beginning of *Dolly* and *dog*. Read the story again. Encourage your child to clap each time he or she hears a word that begins with *d*.

Phonics Skill: Initial Consonant *d*

Dolly does not dig.

Dolly Digs!

by Linda Yoshizawa
illustrated by Remy Simard

Scott Foresman

Editorial Offices: Glenview, Illinois • New York, New York
Sales Offices: Reading, Massachusetts • Duluth, Georgia
Glenview, Illinois • Carrollton, Texas • Menlo Park, California

Dolly digs.
Dad is mad.

No!

Will the dog dig?

Dolly digs.

Dan is mad.

Dan gets a 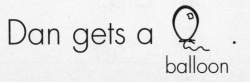 .
balloon

4

Dad digs.

5

Scott Foresman
Reading

Kindergarten
Phonics Reader 21

Lemons and Lions
by Susana Vasquez
illustrated by
Lynn Titleman

Phonics Skills:
• Initial consonant /

Scott Foresman
Phonics System

Scott Foresman

Lemons and Lions

by Susana Vasquez
illustrated by Lynn Titleman

This book belongs to

_____

Phonics for Families: This book gives your child practice in reading words that begin with *l*, as in *lion*, and the high-frequency words *one* and *what*. Read the book together. Then ask your child to find words in the story that begin with *l*.

Phonics Skill: *l*

High-Frequency Words: *one, what*

like to drink lemonade!

Lemons and Lions

by Susana Vasquez
illustrated by Lynn Titleman

Scott Foresman

Editorial Offices: Glenview, Illinois • New York, New York
Sales Offices: Reading, Massachusetts • Duluth, Georgia
Glenview, Illinois • Carrollton, Texas • Menlo Park, California

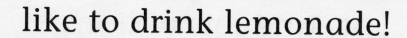

One lemon!

Lots and lots of lions...

Two lions!

Two lemons!

Lots and lots of lemons!

One lion!

Scott Foresman
Reading

Kindergarten
Phonics Reader 22

**Piggy Pop
Went to Shop**
by B.G. Hennessy
illustrated by
Randy Verougstraet

Phonics Skill:
• Short *o*

Scott Foresman
**Phonics
System**

Scott Foresman

by B. G. Hennessy
illustrated by Randy Verougstraet

This book belongs to

_____

Phonics for Families: This book gives your child practice reading words with short *o* in the word families *-ot* and *-op*. Read the book together. Then have your child say words that rhyme with *mop* and *pot*.

Phonics Skill: Short *o*

Piggy Pop got a lot!

Piggy Pop Went to Shop

by B. G. Hennessy
illustrated by Randy Verougstraet

Scott Foresman

Editorial Offices: Glenview, Illinois • New York, New York
Sales Offices: Reading, Massachusetts • Duluth, Georgia
Glenview, Illinois • Carrollton, Texas • Menlo Park, California

Piggy Pop went to shop.

Piggy Pop was hot!

Piggy Pop got a top.

Piggy Pop got a pot.

Piggy Pop got a cot.

Piggy Pop got a mop.

Scott Foresman
Reading

Kindergarten
Phonics Reader 23

Kids and Kits
by Anastasia Suen

Phonics Skill:
• Initial consonant *k*

Scott Foresman
Phonics System

Scott Foresman

Kids and Kits

by Anastasia Suen

This book belongs to

_____

Phonics for Families: This book features words that begin with the letter *k*, as in *kids* and *kits*, and the high-frequency words *here* and *three*. Invite your child to read the book aloud. Then have him or her name the words in the book that begin with the letter *k* after you.

Phonics Skill: Initial consonant *k*

Featured High-Frequency Words: *here*, *three*

PHOTOGRAPHY Cover, Title Page, Margarette Mead/ The Image Bank; 2, 8 (top), Erwin & Peggy Bauer/Bruce Coleman Inc.; 3, Charles Palek/Animals Animals; 4, Uniphoto Picture Agency; 5, 8 (bottom left), Paul McCormick/The Image Bank; 6, 7, Zig Leszczynski/Animals Animals; 8 (bottom right), Johnny Johnson/Animals Animals.

Three kits!

Three kids!

Three kits!

8

Kids and Kits

by Anastasia Suen

Scott Foresman

Editorial Offices: Glenview, Illinois • New York, New York
Sales Offices: Reading, Massachusetts • Duluth, Georgia
Glenview, Illinois • Carrollton, Texas • Menlo Park, California

Here are three kits.

Three kits hide.

Here are three kits.

Three kits sit.

Here are three kids.

Three kids play.

Scott Foresman
Reading

Kindergarten
Phonics Reader 24

Tag for Two
by Ted Tawara
illustrated by Abby Carter

Phonics Review:
• Consonants
• Short *a*
• Short *i*
• Short *o*

Scott Foresman
Phonics
System

Scott Foresman

Tag for Two

by Ted Tawara
illustrated by Abby Carter

This book belongs to

_____

Phonics for Families: This book helps your child review words with *-an*, *-at*, *-ot*, and *-ig* and the high-frequency words *little* and *two*. Read the book aloud. Then have your child say words that rhyme with *can*, *mat*, *big*, and *not*.

Phonics Review: Word families *-an*, *-at*, *-ot*, and *-ig*

High-Frequency Words: *little, two*

She will run too!

Tag for Two

by Ted Tawara
illustrated by Abby Carter

Scott Foresman

Editorial Offices: Glenview, Illinois • New York, New York
Sales Offices: Reading, Massachusetts • Duluth, Georgia
Glenview, Illinois • Carrollton, Texas • Menlo Park, California

Tag for two!

Dan ran up a big, big hill.

What will Pat do?

Pat ran by the little cat.

Dan did not tag Pat.

Dan ran by the van.

Pat did not tag Dan.

Pat ran by the mat.

Dan did not tag Pat.

Dan ran by the can.

Pat did not tag Dan.

Scott Foresman
Reading

Kindergarten
Phonics Reader 25

Jelly and Jam
by Nat Gabriel
photographed by
Richard Hutchings

Phonics Skill:
• Initial consonant *j*

Scott Foresman
Phonics System

Scott Foresman

Jelly and Jam

by Nat Gabriel
photographed by Richard Hutchings

This book belongs to

_____

Phonics for Families: This book features words that begin with the letter *j*, as in *jelly*, and the high-frequency words *we* and *at*. Read the book with your child. Then help him or her find all the words that begin with the letter *j*.

Phonics Skill: Initial consonant *j*

High-Frequency Words: *at, we*

No jelly? No jam?

We like peanut butter too!

Jelly and Jam

by Nat Gabriel
photographed by Richard Hutchings

Scott Foresman

Editorial Offices: Glenview, Illinois • New York, New York
Sales Offices: Reading, Massachusetts • Duluth, Georgia
Glenview, Illinois • Carrollton, Texas • Menlo Park, California

We like jelly.

We like jam.

Not one jar left?

What can we do?

We look for jelly.

We look for jam.

I jump up.

And so does Sam.

A jar for me!

A jar for Sam!

No more jelly?
Get it at the store!

No more jam?
Just go get more!

Scott Foresman
Reading

Kindergarten
Phonics Reader 26

Wig Is Wet!
by Dina Anastasio
illustrated by
Paul Harvey

Phonics Skill:
• Initial consonant w

Scott Foresman
Phonics System

Scott Foresman

Wig Is Wet!

by Dina Anastasio
illustrated by Paul Harvey

This book belongs to

_____

Phonics for Families: This book features words that begin with *w*, as in *Wig*. Read the book together. Then take a walk around your home, taking turns naming objects whose names begin with *w*.

Phonics Skill: Initial consonant *w*

Yes!

8

Wig Is Wet!

by Dina Anastasio
illustrated by Paul Harvey

Scott Foresman

Editorial Offices: Glenview, Illinois • New York, New York
Sales Offices: Reading, Massachusetts • Duluth, Georgia
Glenview, Illinois • Carrollton, Texas • Menlo Park, California

We see Wig.

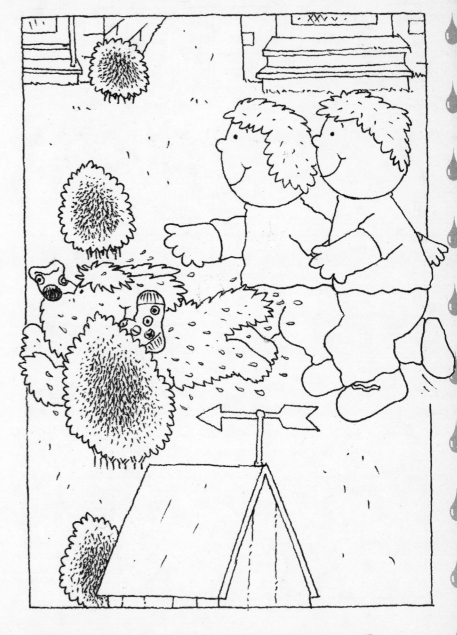

Did Wig get wet here?

Did Wig get wet here?

No!

Wig is wet, wet, wet!

How did Wig get wet?

Did Wig get wet here?

No!

Scott Foresman
Reading

**Kindergarten
Phonics Reader 27**

The Van
by Maryann Dobeck
illustrated by
Rusty Fletcher

Phonics Skill:
• Initial consonant v

Scott Foresman
**Phonics
System**

Scott Foresman

The Van

Move with Vin

by Maryann Dobeck
illustrated by Rusty Fletcher

This book belongs to

_____

Phonics for Families: This book gives your child practice in identifying words that begin with *v*, as in *van*. Read the story aloud. Then encourage your child to find objects in the pictures whose names begin with *v*.

Phonics Skill: Initial consonant *v*

8

The Van

by Maryann Dobeck
illustrated by Rusty Fletcher

Scott Foresman

Editorial Offices: Glenview, Illinois • New York, New York
Sales Offices: Reading, Massachusetts • Duluth, Georgia
Glenview, Illinois • Carrollton, Texas • Menlo Park, California

Vic sees two trucks.

Val sees two ducks.

Who is moving in?

© Scott Foresman K

Val sees two very big dolls.

Vic sees two balls.

4

5

Scott Foresman Reading

Kindergarten
Phonics Reader 28

Jet at the Vet
by Cathy East Dubowski
and Mark Dubowski
illustrated by
Jackie Urbanovic

Phonics Skill:
• Short *e* in word
  families *-et*, *-en*

Scott Foresman Phonics System

Scott Foresman

Jet at the Vet

by Cathy East Dubowski and Mark Dubowski
illustrated by Jackie Urbanovic

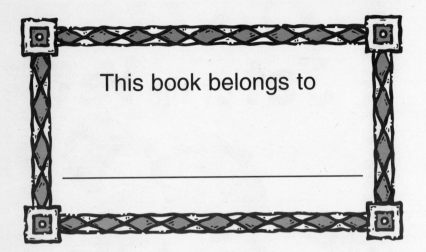

This book belongs to

_____

Phonics for Families: This book features words with *-et* and *-en* and provides practice reading the high-frequency words *you* and *that*. Read the book with your child. Then together, name words that rhyme with the word *vet*.

Phonics Skill: Short *e* in word families *-et, -en*

High-Frequency Words: *that, you*

You bet!

That is why the vet is wet.

8

Jet at the Vet

by Cathy East Dubowski and Mark Dubowski
illustrated by Jackie Urbanovic

Scott Foresman

Editorial Offices: Glenview, Illinois • New York, New York
Sales Offices: Reading, Massachusetts • Duluth, Georgia
Glenview, Illinois • Carrollton, Texas • Menlo Park, California

Ben and Jen have a pet.

Ben and Jen like the vet.

Does Jet like the vet?

The vet likes pets!

They have a big pet!

Here is Jet.

He is the pet.

They all go to the vet.

Jet has not met the vet.

Kindergarten
Phonics Reader 29

**The Queen
and the Quilt**
by Joan Cottle
illustrated by
Luisa D'Augusta

Phonics Skill:
• *qu*

Scott Foresman

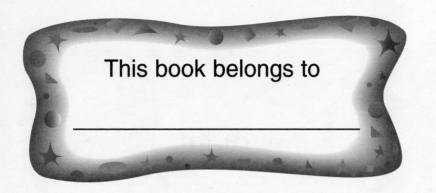

This book belongs to

_____

Phonics for Families: This story provides practice reading words that have the same beginning sound as *queen*. Read the book aloud. Then you and your child can go back through the book and find words that begin with *qu*, as in *queen*.

Phonics Skill: *qu*

The Queen
and
the Quilt

by Joan Cottle

illustrated by Luisa D'Augusta

Scott Foresman

Editorial Offices: Glenview, Illinois • New York, New York
Sales Offices: Reading, Massachusetts • Duluth, Georgia
Glenview, Illinois • Carrollton, Texas • Menlo Park, California

Kindergarten
Phonics Reader 30

Hats
by Anastasia Suen
illustrated by
Lori Osiecki

Phonics Review:
• Consonants
• Short *a*
• Short *e*
• Short *i*
• Short *o*

Scott Foresman

Hats

by Anastasia Suen
illustrated by Lori Osiecki

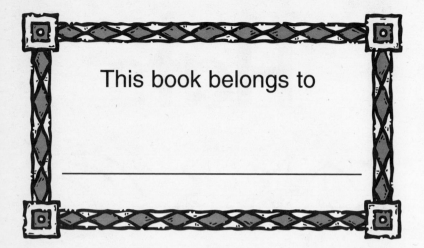

This book belongs to

_____

Phonics for Families: This book provides your child with practice reading words with short *a*, *e*, *i*, and *o* such as *hat*, *get*, *pit*, and *pot*. Invite your child to read the book aloud. Then talk about the hats he or she wears and the activities he or she does when wearing each hat.

Phonics Review: Consonants; Short *a*; Short *e*; Short *i*; Short *o*

Wear a hat.

Have fun!

Hats

by Anastasia Suen
illustrated by Lori Osiecki

Scott Foresman

Editorial Offices: Glenview, Illinois • New York, New York
Sales Offices: Reading, Massachusetts • Duluth, Georgia
Glenview, Illinois • Carrollton, Texas • Menlo Park, California

Wear a hat.

Dig a pit.

Wear a hat.

Hop a lot.

Wear a hat.
Stir a pot.

Wear a hat.
Get a hit.

Wear a hat.

Swim a lap.

Wear a hat.

Take a nap.

Scott Foresman Reading

Kindergarten
Phonics Reader 31

Zebra and the Bug
by Ada Evelyn
illustrated by
Eldon Doty

Phonics Skill:
• Initial and final
  consonants *x, y, z*

Scott Foresman
Phonics System

Scott Foresman

Zebra and the Bug

by Ada Evelyn
illustrated by Eldon Doty

This book belongs to

_____

Phonics for Families: This book provides practice reading words that begin or end with the *x*, *y*, and *z* as in *fox*, *yak*, and *zebra* and provides practice with the high-frequency words *my* and *yellow*. Read the book aloud with your child. Then you and your child can find the words in the story that begin or end with *x*, *y*, and *z*.

Phonics Skill: Initial and final *x*, *y*, *z*

Featured High-Frequency Words: *my*, *yellow*

And my yellow hat is on me!

Zebra and the Bug

by Ada Evelyn
illustrated by Eldon Doty

Scott Foresman

Editorial Offices: Glenview, Illinois • New York, New York
Sales Offices: Reading, Massachusetts • Duluth, Georgia
Glenview, Illinois • Carrollton, Texas • Menlo Park, California

Look!

A bug is on my yellow hat.

No, no, no!
You let it be!

A bug is on my yellow hat.

6

3

Fox wants to hit it.

Ox wants to get it.

Zak wants to zap it.

Yak wants to tap it.

Scott Foresman
Reading

Kindergarten
Phonics Reader 32

Bugs!
by Meish Goldish
illustrated by
Andrea Tachiera

Phonics Skill:
• Short *u*

Scott Foresman
Phonics
System

Scott Foresman

Bugs!

by Meish Goldish
illustrated by Andrea Tachiera

This book belongs to

_____

Phonics for Families: This book gives your child practice in reading words with short *u*, as in *bugs*. Invite your child to read the book aloud. Then together, make up short rhymes with the short *u* words. Example: *A bug is under the rug.*

Phonics Skill: Short *u*

Bugs! Bugs! Bugs!

Bugs!

by Meish Goldish

illustrated by Andrea Tachiera

Scott Foresman

Editorial Offices: Glenview, Illinois • New York, New York
Sales Offices: Reading, Massachusetts • Duluth, Georgia
Glenview, Illinois • Carrollton, Texas • Menlo Park, California

Bugs in a hut!

Bugs on a jug!

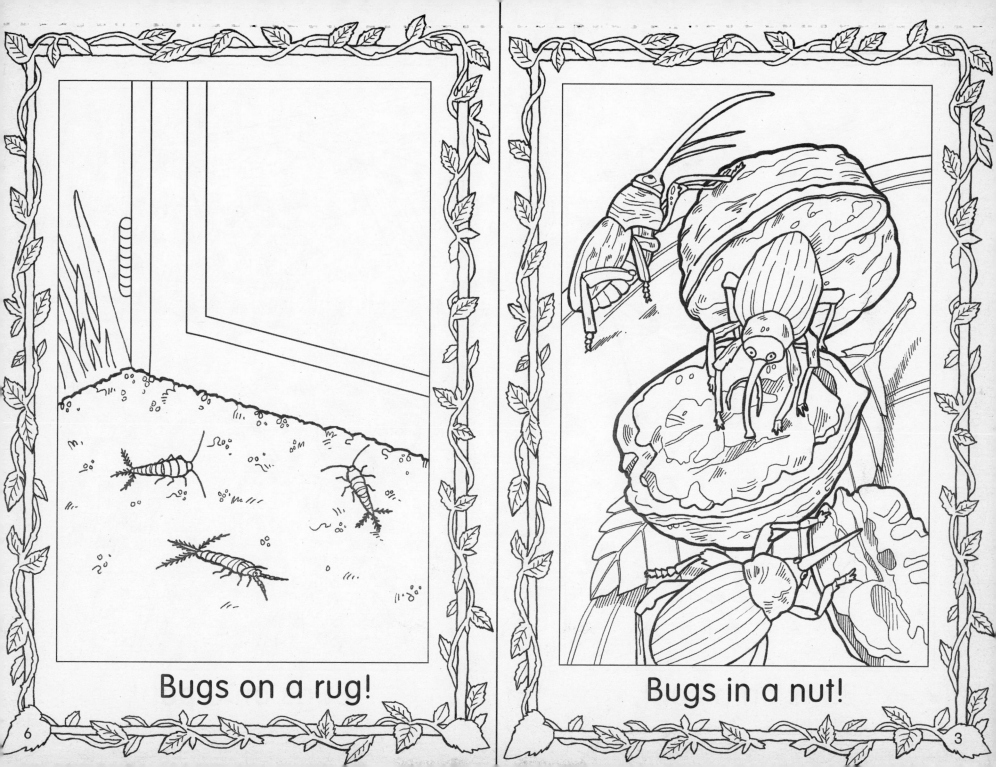

Bugs on a rug!

Bugs in a nut!

6

3

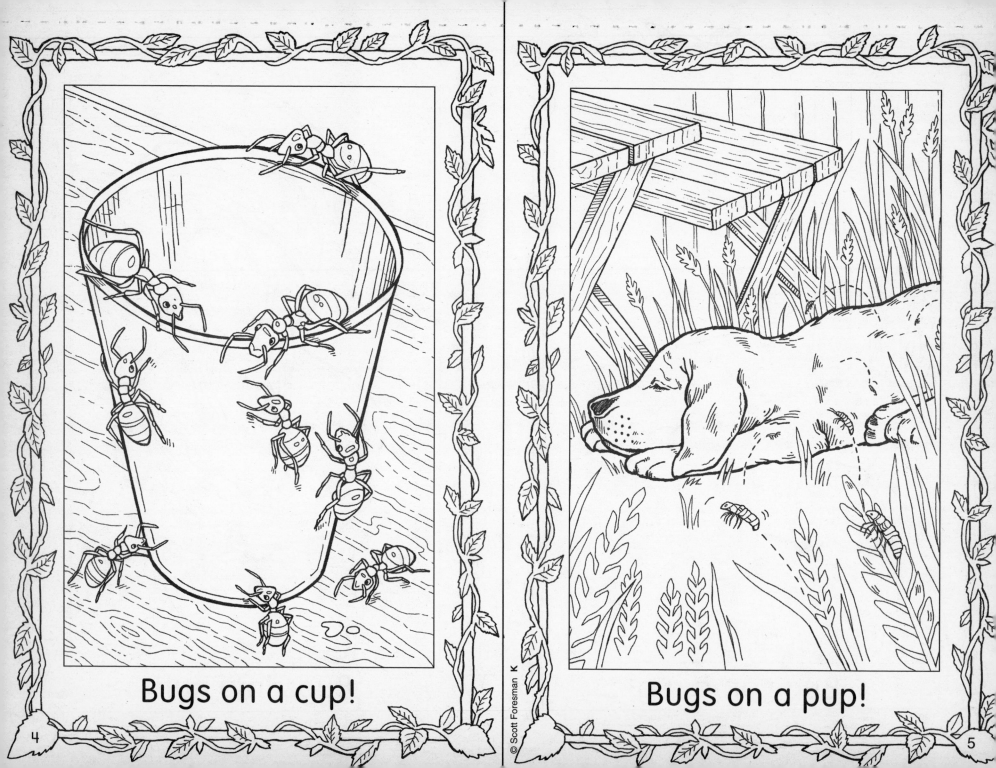

Bugs on a cup!

Bugs on a pup!

4

5

Scott Foresman
Reading

Kindergarten
Phonics Reader 33

Lots and Lots of Dots
by Lucy Floyd
illustrated by
Dan Vascuncellos

Phonics Skill:
• Short vowels

Scott Foresman
Phonics System

Scott Foresman

Lots and Lots of Dots

by Lucy Floyd
illustrated by Dan Vascuncellos

This book belongs to

_____

Phonics for Families: This book reviews words with short vowels, such as *dot, hug,* and *glad,* and provides practice in reading the high-frequency words *see* and *and.* Read the book with your child. Then encourage your child to point out the words with short vowels in the book.

Phonics Skill: Short vowels

High-Frequency Words: *see, and*

Well, you have ten dots!

Pat is glad!

8

Lots and Lots of Dots

by Lucy Floyd

illustrated by Dan Vascuncellos

Scott Foresman

Editorial Offices: Glenview, Illinois • New York, New York
Sales Offices: Reading, Massachusetts • Duluth, Georgia
Glenview, Illinois • Carrollton, Texas • Menlo Park, California

Scott Foresman
Reading

Kindergarten
Phonics Reader 34

What Can Kim Do?
by Linda Yoshizawa
illustrated by
Steve Sanford

Phonics Skill:
• Contrasting long and
  short vowels

Scott Foresman
Phonics
System

Scott Foresman

What Can Kim Do?

by Linda Yoshizawa
illustrated by Steve Sanford

This book belongs to

_____

Phonics for Families: This book gives your child practice in reading words that have short and long vowel sounds, as in *cap* and *cape*, and in reading the high-frequency words *look* and *to*. After reading the story, encourage your child to talk about what he or she likes to do on rainy days.

Phonics Skill: Contrasting long and short vowels

High-Frequency Words: *look, to*

Look, Dad!
I am Kim!

What Can Kim Do?

by Linda Yoshizawa
illustrated by Steve Sanford

Scott Foresman

Editorial Offices: Glenview, Illinois • New York, New York
Sales Offices: Reading, Massachusetts • Duluth, Georgia
Glenview, Illinois • Carrollton, Texas • Menlo Park, California

What can Kim do?

I see tap shoes and a tape.

I like to tap.

I like the tape.

What is in the box?

Mom gets a big box.

6

Scott Foresman
Reading

Kindergarten
Phonics Reader 35

Get That Frog!
by Laurie Lazzaro Knowlton
illustrated by
Tom Garcia

Phonics Skill:
• Initial consonant blends

Scott Foresman
Phonics System

Scott Foresman

Get That Frog!

by Laurie Lazzaro Knowlton
illustrated by Tom Garcia

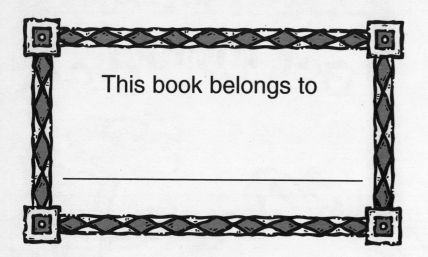

This book belongs to

_____

Phonics for Families: This book provides practice reading words that begin with consonant blends, such as *frog, slip,* and *flat.* Read the book together. Then ask your child to point out the words that begin with consonant blends.

Phonics Skill: Initial consonant blends

8

Get That Frog!

by Laurie Lazzaro Knowlton
illustrated by Tom Garcia

Scott Foresman

Editorial Offices: Glenview, Illinois • New York, New York
Sales Offices: Reading, Massachusetts • Duluth, Georgia
Glenview, Illinois • Carrollton, Texas • Menlo Park, California

A fat frog sat on a log.

Sam slips.
Fred trips.

Pop! The frog is up.

Plop! The frog is down.

Pop! The frog is up.

Plop! The frog is down.

Scott Foresman
Reading

**Kindergarten
Phonics Reader 36**

Sharks
by Kathy Mormile
illustrated by
Jon Weiman

Phonics Review:
• Consonants
• Short vowels
• Initial digraphs

Scott Foresman
Phonics System

Scott Foresman

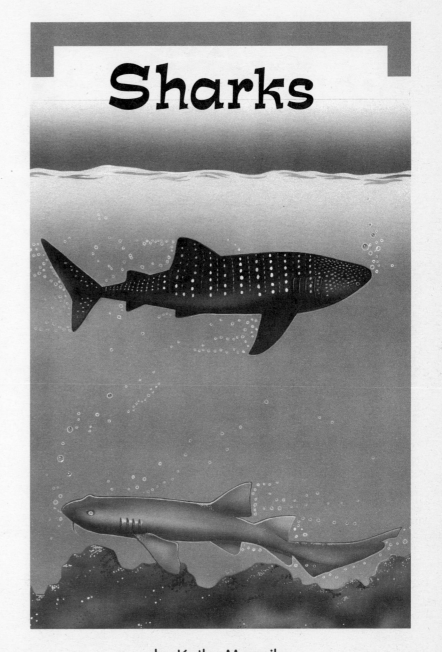

Sharks

by Kathy Mormile
illustrated by Jon Weiman

This book belongs to

_____

© Scott Foresman **K**

Phonics for Families: This book provides practice reading words with short vowels and words with *sh, th,* and *ch,* as in *shark, teeth,* and *chilly.* Read the book together and then invite your child to name other animals that live in the sea whose names begin with contain short vowels and *sh, th,* and *ch.*

Phonics Review: Consonants; Short vowels; Initial digraphs

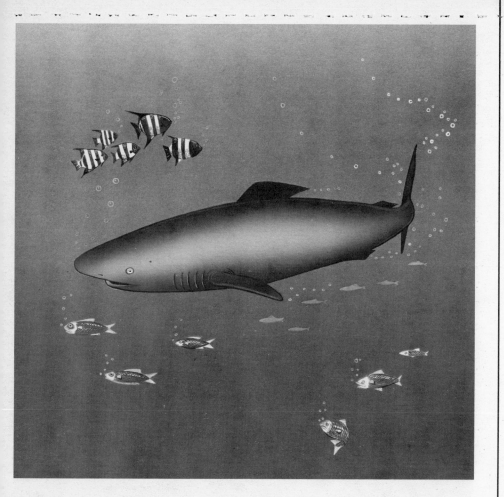

Most sharks live in warm water.

But this shark lives in

chilly water.

But they all swim!

Sharks

by Kathy Mormile
illustrated by Jon Weiman

Scott Foresman

Editorial Offices: Glenview, Illinois • New York, New York
Sales Offices: Reading, Massachusetts • Duluth, Georgia
Glenview, Illinois • Carrollton, Texas • Menlo Park, California

These sharks have small .

teeth

These sharks
like the bottom.

These sharks
like the top.

6

These sharks have big .

teeth

3

This shark is small.

It can fit in your .

hand

This shark is big.

It cannot fit in your .

car